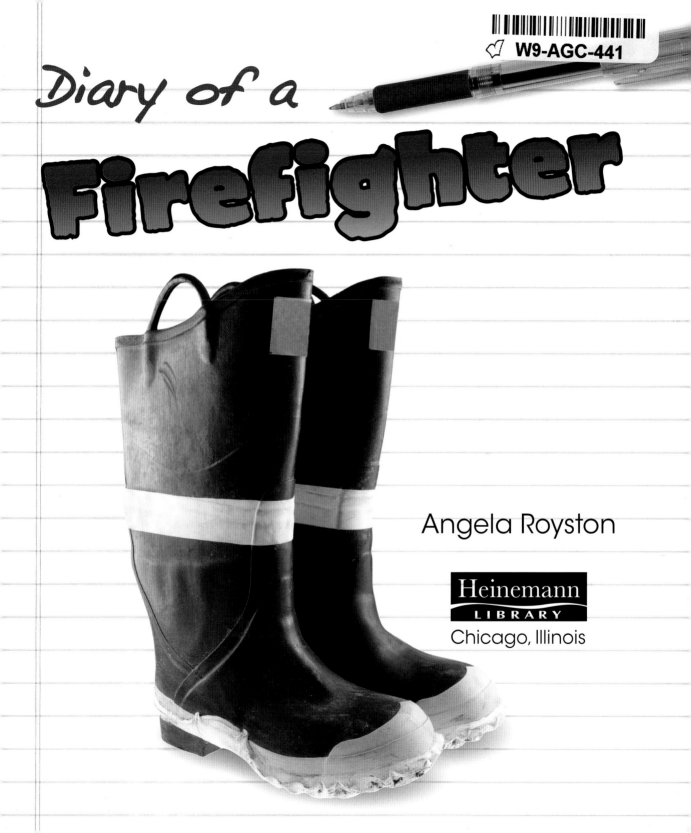

Diary of a Firefighter

Angela Royston

Heinemann
LIBRARY
Chicago, Illinois

To contact Capstone Global Library, please call 800-747-4992,
or visit our web site www.capstonepub.com

Edited by Daniel Nunn, Rebecca Rissman, and Catherine Veitch
Designed by Cynthia Akiyoshi
Picture research by Ruth Blair
Production by Victoria Fitzgerald
Originated by Capstone Global Library Ltd
Printed and bound in China by South China Printing Company Ltd

17 16 15 14 13
10 9 8 7 6 5 4 3 2 1

Library of Congress Cataloging-in-Publication Data
Royston, Angela, 1945-
 Firefighter / Angela Royston.
  pages cm.—(Diary of a...)
 Includes bibliographical references and index.
 ISBN 978-1-4329-7583-8 (hb)—ISBN 978-1-4329-7590-6 (pb)
 1. Fire extinction—Juvenile literature. 2. Fire fighters—Juvenile
literature. I. Title. II. Title: Fire fighter.
 TH9148.R753 2014
 363.37—dc23
                           2012046861

Acknowledgments
We would like to thank the following for permission to reproduce
photographs: Corbis pp. 6 (© Creasource), 7 (© George Hall),
9 (© Julien Thomazo/Photononstop), 17 (© John O'Boyle/
Star Ledger), 20 (© Andrew Aitchison/In Pictures), 22 (© Ramin
Talaie), 25 (© Stan Carroll/ZUMA Press), 26 (© Uden Graham/
Redlink), 5; Getty Images pp. 4 (Peter Macdiarmid), 12 (Jac
Depczyk), 14 (YURI CORTEZ/AFP), 15 (Alain Le Bot), 16 (Adam
Berry); Shutterstock pp. title page (© L Barnwell), contents page
(© John Kasawa), 8 (© PerseoMedusa), 13 (© Brian McDonald),
18 (© Andreev Alexey), 19 (© TFoxFoto), 21 (© Taras Kolomiyets),
28 (© FWStudio); Superstock pp. 10 (Radius), 11 (Stockbroker /
Purestock), 23, 24 (imagebroker.net), 27 (Ambient Images Inc.).

Background and design features reproduced with permission
of Shutterstock. Cover photograph of firefighter next to fire
reproduced with permission of Shutterstock (© Digital Storm).

We would like to thank Mark Oddi for his invaluable help in the
preparation of this book.

Every effort has been made to contact copyright holders of
material reproduced in this book. Any omissions will be rectified in
subsequent printings if notice is given to the publisher.

All the Internet addresses (URLs) given in this book were valid at
the time of going to press. However, due to the dynamic nature
of the Internet, some addresses may have changed, or sites may
have changed or ceased to exist since publication. While the
author and publisher regret any inconvenience this may cause
readers, no responsibility for any such changes can be accepted
by either the author or the publisher.

Some words are shown in bold, **like this**. You can find
out what they mean by looking in the Glossary.

Contents

Ready to Go

Monday, October 2

My days as a firefighter are all so different that I've decided to keep a diary. I'm in the **fire station** now, drinking a cup of coffee—but I'm ready if the alarm goes off.

I always work with the same group of
firefighters. When we came on duty this
morning, we checked the fire engine
and all the equipment. We know that
everything is in working order.

Called into Action

As I was writing in my diary, the alarm went off! Quickly, I slid down the pole and climbed into the fire engine. I put on my hat and jacket as we raced to the fire.

6

When we got there, we found it was a false alarm. We went into the building and checked every room carefully. Someone had seen smoke, but nothing was burning.

Fire Safety

Tuesday, October 3

A big part of my job is preventing fires. This morning I visited a restaurant to check that it is safe. We checked the kitchen, the **fire doors**, and the **fire exits**.

This sign points to the fire exit.

I also tested the **smoke alarms** on each floor and made sure they were attached in the right places. Smoke alarms beep loudly as soon as any smoke reaches them. They let people know that they have to get out.

Safety First

Safety is the most important part of our job. We save people before we worry about property. We keep ourselves safe, too. Our clothes are made of special material that does not catch fire.

helmet

breathing apparatus

fire-resistant material

We use a **breathing apparatus** whenever we go into a burning building. It gives us clean air to breathe and protects us from smoke and gases.

Real Emergency

Wednesday, October 4

We had a real emergency today. A mother and child were trapped in a burning apartment. The **sirens** screeched as we raced through the traffic.

We could see the flames even before we arrived. I got the hose out and started spraying the flames. Then several other fire engines arrived.

Rescue

Two of our firefighters went into the building and up to the apartment. There was smoke everywhere, but they managed to find the woman and the child.

By this time, the long ladder was in place. Five minutes later, the two **casualties** were on the ground, safe and sound. It took much longer to put the fire out!

Learning on the Job

Thursday, October 5

A new **recruit** named Sharon joined us at the station today. She has already had official training, so she knows how to use the equipment.

A firefighter practices rescuing with a dummy.

Meeting her made me remember my first day at the **fire station**. I couldn't wait to put what I had learned into practice! My very first job was to help pump floodwater out of a basement.

A Routine Kind of Day

Friday, October 6

Sharon, the new **recruit**, came with me to visit a school this morning. I told the children how to keep themselves safe from fire.

I told the children never to play with matches.

Sharon told them about her training and how firefighters cannot be afraid of heights. They also have to be good at talking to people. She did a great job—the children loved her!

Fire Practice

In the afternoon, we practiced a **fire drill**. We do drills all the time. We get to know them so well that we do not have to stop and think in an emergency.

Then we had a session called "know your streets." This was helpful for Sharon. We went through all the local hazards we knew about, such as old, empty buildings.

Chemical Spill

Saturday, October 7

We had another big emergency today. A truck carrying barrels of dangerous **chemicals** crashed on the highway. Some of the chemicals spilled across the road.

We put on **biohazard suits** to protect ourselves from the chemicals.

Police and fire crews were already there when we arrived. They had **cordoned off** the road and stopped the traffic. We wore **breathing apparatuses** to protect us from breathing in any chemicals.

Dealing with Danger

Dealing with **chemicals** and other hazards takes lots of special training. Chemicals can be dangerous to people and the environment.

This special sprayer gets our suits really clean!

We cleaned up the spill and made the rest of the barrels safe. Then our suits were washed down. We had to make sure there were no dangerous chemicals on our clothes.

Where Next?

Sunday, October 8

I had a day off at last and some time to plan my future. What do I want to do? I could apply to join a fire crew at an airport.

I could specialize in fighting forest fires, but I'd have to leave the city. If I stay where I am, I might be put in charge of a group of firefighters. One day I could even become a fire chief.

Writing a Diary

Firefighters at the **fire station** keep a log of everything that happens. The log **records** the time and reason that each fire engine is called. This book is a diary. It tells what happened from the firefighter's point of view.

You can write a diary, too! Your diary can describe your life—what you saw, what you felt, and the events that happened.

Here are some tips for writing a diary:

 Start each entry with the day and the date. You don't have to include an entry for every day.

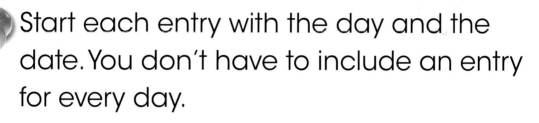 The entries should be in **chronological** order, which means that they follow the order in which events happened.

Use the past tense when you are writing about something that has already happened.

 Remember that a diary is the writer's story, so use "I" and "my."

Glossary

biohazard suit special clothes worn for dealing with something dangerous

breathing apparatus mask, pipe, and supply of air

casualty person hurt in an accident

chemical solid, liquid, or gas that is used to make something. Some chemicals are harmful.

chronological in order of time

cordoned off closed to the public by a piece of tape or a barrier

fire door door that does not burn easily and so helps to stop a fire from spreading

fire drill set of actions relating to fire safety that are repeated again and again

fire exit way out of a building if there is a fire

fire resistant does not catch fire

fire station building where fire engines and equipment are kept and where firefighters work and stay when on duty

record write something down for later use

recruit someone who has only just become a firefighter

siren machine that makes a loud noise to catch people's attention

smoke alarm device that beeps very loudly when smoke reaches it

Find Out More

Books

Aylmore, Angela. *We Work at the Fire Station* (Where We Work). Chicago: Heinemann Library, 2006.

Daynes, Katie. *Firefighters* (Usbourne Beginners). Tulsa, Okla.: EDC, 2007.

Mortensen, Lori. *A Day at the Fire Station* (First Graphics: My Community). Mankato, Minn.: Capstone, 2011.

Pipe, Jim. *Fire Engines* (Read and Play). Mankato, Minn.: Stargazer, 2009.

Internet sites

Facthound offers a safe, fun way to find Internet sites related to this book. All of the sites on Facthound have been researched by our staff.

Here's all you do:
Visit www.facthound.com
Type in this code: 9781432975838

Index